SONGS OF THE GOOD EARTH

D1548133

Best Wishes
Margaret Phillips

Other Books by Margaret I. Phillips:

Doctor of the Cotton Patch, 1968
The Governors of Tennessee, 1978

Songs
of the
Good Earth

Margaret I. Phillips

PELICAN PUBLISHING COMPANY
GRETNA 1980

Library of Congress Cataloging in Publication Data

Phillips, Margaret I.
   Songs of the good Earth.

    1. Meditations. 2. Phillips, Margaret I.
I. Title.
BV 4832.2.P498   242   79-10731
ISBN 0-88289-221-5

Some of the material in this work was adapted
from an article by the author in *Farm Journal* and
from her columns in the following newspapers:
News Courier, Athens, Alabama; *Florence Times-
Daily* and *Florence Herald Picture,* Florence,
Alabama; *Democrat-Union,* Lawrenceburg, Tennessee; and *Giles Free Press* in Pulaski, Tennessee.

Manufactured in the United States of America

Published by Pelican Publishing Company, Inc.
1101 Monroe Street, Gretna, Louisiana 70053

That I may publish with the voice of thanksgiving, and tell of all thy wondrous works. (Psalms 26:7)

Contents

Preface

I stood on a windy hill and listened to spring's approaching sounds. I heard a rippling brook overflowing its banks because of moisture in the earth no longer frozen. I listened to the sound of chattering blackbirds nestling in the barren treetops that were just ready to bring forth their buds. I glanced across the soft earth and saw a greenness pushing upward that hadn't been there before; and just as I was about to say goodbye to winter, I heard the sound of wild geese overhead. I heeded their anxious cry. They were disturbed, no doubt, by gunshot from a hunter whom they had escaped. Their formation was broken, and they flew awkwardly through the air—quite low for wild geese.

I stood there, silhouetted against a red sunset, and pondered the sound I detected in their cries. Was it fear? Anxiety? Eagerness? It seemed a mixture of all as I hearkened to their gaping call. But no matter, they flew steadily onward, each finding its own way in its struggle for survival.

Just like humans, thought I, as I watched their flight—each of us in our own way struggling for existence in whatever walk of life we have chosen, for it does take struggling if we are to accomplish anything in the end; if, like the wild goose, we find our way homeward. . . .

Anyway, happy springtime, reader friends, or happy any season whether in fair weather or foul, and may you find insight into the joys and strengths obtained from the association with the land as you explore the pages of this book.

Spring

Spring! And I wish there were two of me—one to do all the things that I want to do and the other to do all the things that I must do! There would be one of me to take a seven-year-old by the hand and say, "Okay, Son, let's go fishing today! The painting can wait."

All day I would revel in shared confidences; rejoice as I looked deep into the eyes of youth with their clear sparkle, unhurt as yet by the world and its experiences, at evening time to walk slowly homeward with the feeling of love and warmth around my heart, and memories to treasure always.

To the silent but quickly growing grass in my back yard I would urge, "Go back! Stay there in the dampness of your earthbed. We are too busy to bother with you out here in the world of sunlight and beauty...."

Let there be time for laughter today, Spring. Time for a tea party with a wee four-year-old; time to answer a million questions: "How many miles from here to the moon, Mom?"; "What means *Bless*, Mommie?"; "Now, Mom, is there *really* a Santa Claus?"; "How far *down* does our land go, Mom?"; "But we don't have war in our country, do we, Mom?"; "Why must good people get killed just because bad people do,

Mom?"; "Did Jesus send that, Mommie?" when the storm had passed on.

But most of all, Spring, let there be time for love. Time for sharing, and especially time for caring. And surely let me be not afraid, Spring, to bask in this good life. Let there be time to reach out my hand to Him who "madest Earth and Heaven," so beautiful and so magnificent, and ask that He make me lovely too. Not outwardly—I would not be so vain—but inwardly, that He might let me grow so that I can embrace not only my little group of family and friends (for may my friendship with others not end at my doorstep) but go far into a waiting world. Then I can know that I have shared with others that which He has given me here on the land.

Thus, in such fulfillment, I am committed to my typewriter in spring as perhaps at no other season as I absorb the wealth of nature's bounties and clasp them to my heart: the birds that sing with a sweeter lilt, the seeping message of earth speaking to us in mellow tones as the clammy cloak of winter is chased away by the warm rays of the sun, and the quiet accents of nature's patient waiting can be heard—the steady buzzing of small insects, the gentle stirring of leaves grown suddenly full and green. And I am aware of the fact that once again, even though I have watched closely, I have missed the miraculous unfolding of the season.

Each year I remind myself—now this year, watch! This year, be sure that you catch the magnificent drama, the surreptitious unfolding of spring. First, from the barren tree the bud, and then overnight almost, the leaf. So this year, watch! Things just can't happen that swiftly, not right before your eyes.

But even so, the season eludes me with its mysterious performance. One day I observe the trees in our back pasture—the dogwood's pictorial beauty; the redbud's sanguine cloud; the silverleaf's unfledged foliage, its maturity nearest in sight; the sugar maple, usually later in its array of green than its neighbors, pregnant with its own potential of plumage. The very next day I look again, keeping my constant vigil. But it has happened again! The leaves on the trees are full in their splendor and the miracle is again lost to my sight.

And I apply a bit of my philosophy to nature's drama which is synonymous with life itself, for in spring's early leaf we see a reflection of our own "short hour," and confronted by my young who are ever on the move as they run and laugh and play, I am again aware of nature at work in the unfolding of their jubilant lives.

So watch, I again remind myself. Be aware of nature and her work. Also watch *them* grow. Observe each change, each additional inch in height. Evaluate each depth in understanding, each volume of maturation; like the early leaf of spring I have learned that the leaf of my young is just as ephemeral.

Therefore this book, with its recorded conversations with my son and daughter, captured at various stages of their growth—disclosing in dialogue lessons learned from that great teacher, the land—lessons reflected in every season, for each one has left to us its gift.

On the land, we have known joy and happiness; and we have known sorrow as well. We yielded to the discipline of "constant adversity"—our private pun for the chores that demanded our attention twice each day—but we learned the value of that discipline at evening time which meant home and love, suppertime, and the family circle.

Quiet walks let us share the common things around us, for we knew if we were generous in explaining small things, our young would be better prepared for the bigger things ahead; for just as the earth brings forth living organisms dependent upon the growth of other organisms for their survival, so must our culture depend upon the interactions of human beings for its survival.

Above all, I hope their life on the land will have taught our young the true meaning of the word "weed"; and having learned it, may they have determined to become useful plants instead.

"Why'd they put Him on the cross, Daddy?" our youngest asked as the Easter season approached. It was one of those appalling moments when I experienced a sort of compassion for my mate and at the same time a secret thankfulness that he, rather than I, was at the helm of explanation, for an answer must be found satisfying the curiosity of youth without causing undue emotional tremors at so early an age. Above all, the greater need of impressing the true meaning of the season must be met.

So I listened as my child's daddy told her the story of the crucifixion; a story too deep for a six-year-old to understand, but a story which, if left unexplained, might lead her to conclude that the only meaning of Easter was the new white dress hanging in her closet, the shiny new shoes she was expecting, and the visit from the Easter Bunny that still came around in her young world.

I thought of my own youthful misgivings regarding the season of Easter, especially those involving Good Friday, for indeed in my own life—as it will no doubt be in the life of my young—it has taken maturity to comprehend the irony in the fact that the gruesome Friday on which the Savior of mankind was executed could have become commemorated to posterity as "Good Friday." The connotation of the paradox exemplifies the season, for without a winter there could follow no springtime; without a death, no resurrection; without an awareness of persons who have winter souls there would be no appreciation for those who smile through tears and march steadily through hardships, remaining optimistic individuals who are sure that there is a brighter side to life because man, too, is part divine, his visage upward.

Thus the Christian at this season seeks communication with the resurrected Savior, and the fulfillment of a life that is less burdened while experiencing his own inner resurrection. For winter, whether in the earth's seasons or in the heart's emotions, has a way of arriving too soon and must be tempered by the gentle winds of hope. So then must the crucified Body, broken and bruised on that fateful Friday, come alive on another day to cleanse the ugliness that comes too quickly into an apathetic world.

Spring marks the beginning of a new year, a growing year, when shoots of new life struggle and stand erect, though bitten back at times by the aftermath of a blustery winter. If one looks closely, in nature as in man, there is discovered that push, that drive that evokes the effort for life.

So it is fitting, and possibly planned, that the Easter season elicits such a mood in all creation, man and nature alike. At this new beginning, when the old is cast aside and a crisp newness starts, we see the world around us burst forth in its new inception, and we feel it in the relationship between neighbors and friends in springtime.

To my daughter's impression of this great season, whatever it might have been as she listened to her dad, I found myself wanting to add: Now watch, Child. Look every day for this newness that spreads itself before your eyes, that creeps into your heart at this season, that gives to you a warm association with nature and, as you grow older, your fellowman.

A bit of seriousness, a good deal of gaiety, and a large slice of truth are the requirements in this job of parenthood.

My favorite rose bush is heavy with its burden of blooms— so huge its blossoms, so deep its color. Fragrant with an air of nostalgia about it, I wondered, as I held a petal close to my nostrils, why it should affect me in such a manner.

I hadn't damaged the huge, clinging vine by pruning its

branches so close last fall. Beneath the force of my shears, each stem had crushed quietly without so much as a flinch, fighting not its destiny. But I hadn't cut away too much, for here was my result, a fuller, more beautiful blossom.

I studied the blossom and I thought about life. How very much pruning our own lives require at times in order for something more beautiful to shine through. Sometimes we may feel that we receive a little more cutting away than is necessary for our well-being, and, unlike the rose, we are not so easily pruned. We do not accept the wielding of the shears in so humble a manner, but stubbornly cling to those traits that make up our personalities.

Like the rose, we sometimes find our own blossom stunted by the growth of thorns and, in the end, we come out better persons by the use of our Master's shears. When we have shed the thorns of selfishness, indifference, and intolerance, a richer fuller blossom can be found. Yet patience is not an easy thing to learn in the life of the adult or the child, and here again, nature takes us to task and reveals to us in her simple analogies a greater truth.

I encountered our youngest, when she was four, as she stood by my favorite chrysanthemum, slowly picking the buds just ready to bloom. Her tiny blue jean pockets were bulging with the little buds when I came upon her unexpectedly.

Seeing the favorite flower (it had been given to me by a friend during a bout at the hospital and replanted in my yard) void of its buds, my reaction had been a bit on the extreme as I reprimanded my daughter for her actions. Then, realizing that I had spoken too sharply, I dropped to her level on bended knees, and together we opened one of the tiny green buds from her pocket. She watched, fascinated, as I slowly removed the tight green covering, revealing tiny blossoms not yet grown. She listened intently as I explained the process through which they developed, and was saddened as I helped her to understand that in plucking the buds too soon she was destroying a thing of beauty.

As I talked to my daughter, a thought occurred to me: we grown-ups are so like children ourselves. How many things of beauty do we destroy daily in the lives of those around us when we, as my four-year-old had done, pluck the buds too soon? How much ugliness could be turned into beauty with a different approach to a situation? How much more patient could we be in handling our problems if we were willing to wait for full bloom instead of tiring ourselves out trying to solve them before they matured? For sometimes, with the waiting for maturity, we find not a problem, but a blossom.

It was not an unusual day. It started off with the birth of Spot's kittens. We didn't find the kittens at once, but our youngsters are keen observers. They could tell at a glance that nature had climaxed her handiwork. It was a Saturday, the first yard-cutting day of the year. Eggshells popped up here and there on the thick sod of green grass where unfound Easter eggs had not escaped the lawn mower's blade. A baby rabbit scurried from its warm furry bed, but failed to make it past our nine-year-old and wound up in the empty parakeet cage.

Our youngest was away for the day; so was her dad.

"Walk with me to get the cows, Mom," my son invited, since it fell his turn to bring in the Holsteins from the grass at noon.

I know an opportunity—sometimes—when I see one, and here I had two of them: a chance to hurry through my housework undisturbed or a chance to share a walk rich in fellowship with my son. I chose the latter.

We took our camera along for we never knew what unexpected beautiful scenes nature would have for us—a pair of

Holstein heifers with heads poked out the paneless windows of an ancient log house that stands in our pasture was the first snapshot taken—my son couldn't resist! And then we stopped to talk about that old log house and its past, with its sagging floors where numerous tiny feet had romped and played; its broken windows, with glass gone now, where tiny noses had spent hours pressed tight against cold window panes as wistful young faces peered out into the winter cold; its fallen chimney, where warmth from the open fireplace had sparked many an after-dinner conversation in years past, where flickering firelight embers had engulfed many hopes and dreams.

We couldn't dare guess the old house's age, but my son was amused at the initials that were cut into the many trees that grew around it. I know not the origin of the initials, but I explained that in some way, the people whose initials were cut into the bark had played a part in the life of the old house. Perhaps the persons had lived there once, or visited there as children at play; perhaps the initials connotated a deeper relationship than that of friendship. Surely the old house had touched the lives of many people in its years of existence, both their joys and their sorrows.

Then I related to my son the only occasion in which I had contributed anything to the spirit of the old house—when I was a young bride in our own home, a family lived in the old house and the only child in the home, a tiny four-year-old girl, died. The mother was concerned that her little daughter's favorite doll—which was to accompany the child in her long sleep—had no shoes and that its little dress was soiled. The neighbor women had laundered the dress, and I had hurried to our own house and from stiffened white material made a tiny pair of doll shoes with pink ribbon bows.

That, as I recalled, had been my only contribution to the old house, or its history of inhabitants, that stands there in our pasture, used now for a hay shed. Now the only visible signs of life that exist near the old building are the black and white Holsteins.

We continued with our walk across the shady valley with its scent of spring and growing things; mint, growing along the brook's edge, freshly washed from the rain the night before, penetrated our nostrils. Long blades of grass glistened in the noonday sun and squashed beneath our feet as we made our way along. Our brook was a bit out-of-bounds, but a log made a good crossing as we carefully balanced our weight, placing first one foot straight with the slippery wet log, and then the other, while behind us walked our shepherd dog, just as carefully, with his head held high in constant alertness lest we make a bad footing and land in the rushing water below.

Fuzzy yellow worms covered the trunk of a huge locust tree, but this snap we had to leave—too much shade. The cows refused to wait for us at the pond, so we missed a snap of them where they usually stopped and encircled the clear blue pool in their thirst for fresh water.

We had walked slowly on the way, and as we walked, we talked. We talked of home, of friends, of school. I learned my son's conception of what flying saucers "really were"; how birds' nests should not be touched by human hands; of his friendship with the shepherd, who usually occupied the place by his side where I stood today; and that he really did like Saturdays at home.

My gaping vacuum cleaner greeted me upon our return, but I knew, come my tomorrows, I would forget the unswept floors, recalling only the warm touch of a firm young hand, with a shepherd trailing in the distance. . . .

"Now, Mommie, don't cut off too much," our youngest complained, referring to the evergreens around our house, for she was a sentimentalist at the tender age of seven and wanted nothing that she loved changed.

"Oh, yes," I carefully explained, "they have grown too

large and they will soon ruin if I don't cut them back to a smaller size."

As I spoke to my daughter, I realized that I was voicing a lesson in chastisement, so I volunteered further, "People are like that too you know."

"How do you trim people back, Mommie?"

"With discipline. When we are little and we get naughty, as little people sometimes do, then parents and teachers must use discipline to control us. Otherwise, we grow into ornery adults."

"Oh," she replied wonderingly, looking up into my face.

"When we grow up and become adults, and get too big and smart, then the Lord has a way of taking care of us, too, by His own methods of discipline, trimming us back a bit so that we don't get in the same shape as the shrubbery."

"Then I guess the Lord should trim [name] down some, don't you think so, Mommie?"

I tried not to let my amusement show as I got a mental vision of the character she had mentioned.

"I'm afraid I might like to agree with you, honey. But if I do then we will be judging, and I understand we are not supposed to do that, either."

Again, an "oh" escaped, this time clearly revealing the disappointment she felt. After all, what kind of world was she living in if she couldn't make up her own mind about the people she encountered?

I dug on in the rich soil around the shrubbery, crumbling the loose grains of earth, heaping it around the deep roots, glad of it and the lessons it reminded me to teach those around me.

The farmer's agrarian policy of preserving plants at all cost is often in gross contrast to that other ethical value learned on the land—the protection of animal life. To the Epicurean young, no life is worthless if it belongs to the animal kingdom, and even the common house fly and the spider have had their cases pled at our house as I held the fly flap in mid-air. At times, values become a bit complex, and require, at best, some compromising, if we are not to uproot those other values so painstakingly taught already.

I recall a day in April—one of those days that brought out the gardener in me and in my youngsters as well. I've noticed since that the desire for the hoe lessens with the years, in the young and the middle aged alike, but on the day that I am writing about the urge was still present. At our house it revealed Flopsy, Mopsy, Cottontail, and Pete; however, at the time of the discovery it was a bit hard to determine which was which. It hardly seemed feasible, in fact, that any of the four smooth-rumped little fellows would turn out to be Cottontail!

Our youngest came upon them first as she was giving me her assistance with the flower beds. "Eek!" she squealed, holding her wire rack in mid-air as the brown, shiny heads began to bob up and down in the hole that she had unearthed. At her shriek I rushed forward, my hoe raised for the kill for I was sure that she had uncovered a vicious viper.

"Mom! It's baby rabbits!" our eldest screamed at me from behind.

I slackened my grip on the hoe and peered closer as my youngsters dropped on bended knees beside the little fellows with eyes closed, all wound up into a ball.

"Rabbits without fur?" I questioned.

"Oh, Mom! They're only babies," my son insisted, and warned his sister in his next breath not to touch them.

"Their mother might not claim them again if she can smell human scent. Birds won't, they say."

So gently we wrapped Flopsy, Mopsy, Cottontail, and Pete back in their fur-mingled mound of grass in the center of our flower bed, and all the while I was eyeing my cabbage row in the vegetable garden not twenty feet away. Now I knew what had stripped off the leaves from my young cabbage plants two weeks after we had planted them! The leaves had grown a second time, but how long would the tender young shoots stay that way when this family began to prowl? But how could I explain to my young that sharp blades of steel across soft backs of fur was logical reasoning in anyone's culture—agrarian or otherwise.

"Oh, for heavens sake!" said my farmer-husband (that was not the exact term he used, but it looks better here), "I didn't order extra-large-flats, I told them to send medium-flat seed corn. Hey Mom! Have you got business in town this morning?"

Town to us is the shopping center some twenty miles away. I could think of a couple of errands that I should do—checking on my typewriter in the shop was one thing—so I was elected for returning three bags of seed corn before the planter caught up with them.

"Now hurry!" said my busy spouse.

He knew I had never done that in my life! I couldn't really hurry this day, either. It was one of the nicest morning drives that I had taken during the spring, for I love early mornings in June. Tractors were humming and young plants were shooting forth from the earth in long straight rows. Homemakers were sweeping porches and walkways and digging in flower beds and vegetable gardens. Dairy herds grazed in new summer pastures and farmers slashed away with mowers and rakes at the remains of the old. Who could hurry through such tranquility?

Then, I thought of other lands and other problems: noises other then the tractor's purr; digging not that of the gardener;

emotional twinges to stir the heart of the observer other than the surge of contentment which filled my own. I remembered a conversation with our youngest just the day before.

"Mommie, are we about to have war?" she asked, looking up into my face through troubled blue eyes that keenly revealed the disturbance she felt within her heart.

"I hope not, dear," I answered.

"Mommie, if we do have war, will our side win?"

"Of course, honey. We're the strongest nation in the world."

"Mommie, what if we don't have enough ammunition to win?"

"We've got enough," I had assured her, as I placed my arm around troubled shoulders and urged that she not worry about such things; there were other ways to work out our country's problems without going to war, I felt sure!

She has learned in her young world that when she dispels her anxieties upon me, they subside. I know of her apprehensions, but she knows not of mine. How can she know that even though I may bring calmness to her own world, there is little I can do about my own?

I turn my eyes upward. The heavens are blue and clear; no sign of destruction there. Somewhere, in that great beyond, or in the very presence of self—wherein He dwells I am not sure yet—is my own comforter. I search for Him, and He is there. He knows my own fears and of the troubled Middle East, as well as of our peaceful countryside.

"Bring me your burdens," He has invited, and I do.

We watched Saturn Five's historic blast-off from Cape Kennedy. Dad watched, too, as this heaviest machine ever to leave the earth began its journey. I had a feeling though that he was more concerned with the amount of money the lofty endeavor was costing the government and the fact that his watching was going to cause a delay in his morning milking schedule than with the good this mission might do mankind. He has his feet firmly planted on the good earth and makes it plain that he intends to keep them there.

Our youngest wasn't too concerned about either—the dairy herd or Saturn Five's launch. She was more aware of the fact that she had left her house slippers down the hall in her bedroom. Pulling her feet up under her warm granny gown, she snuggled close to her dad on the couch and made up, in part, for the sleep she was missing in order to watch this eventful blast-off that, according to her brother, was to be something special.

Our eldest, all bright-eyed and bushy haired—who insisted that the whole family witness this event—took us orally through the procedure of the launching process. In his eagerness he got a bit ahead of the news commentator at times until it was impossible to hear either of them, both of whom thrilled greatly to the fact that everything got off as scheduled.

Our son hasn't quite made up his mind about this earth-space business, possessing a keen interest in each. At the age of five he revealed to us that his future ambition was to be a farmer-astronaut. I wasn't at all sure what a farmer-astronaut would be, so I found it a bit hard to give my heartiest approval to his ambitions. Yet I declined encouragement with a guilty feeling; after all, I might be hampering the progress of science by discouraging the world's first farmer-astronaut! A farmer-astronaut just might not be what I had imagined—a part time space man delving around in the soil at other times. A farmer-astronaut might just be one who went down instead of up. Of course, he might have to change his title a bit, but I could imagine a vast store of information for the world, not to mention its rich resources, beneath the earth's sod. Now my conscience hurt me even worse at the disillusion I may have unintentionally offered such endeavors, for I understand we are becoming concerned with "inner space" as well as the outer type, and that it may become our next frontier of science. So who am I to say that a farmer-astronaut would not earn a place in history for himself!

No wonder I felt even more ashamed when our eldest—with five years added to his growth since first he broached me with his ambitions—asked, "Mom, do you know how many miles *down* our land goes?"

I sadly shook my head. To tell the truth, I had never thought about it. All I ever planned on, in depth that is, was about six feet.

"Mom, why don't you write something for little people sometime?" my youngest recently requested, "and use words that we can pronounce."

So this, my child, is for you, as June approaches and the graduating high school seniors look out into our faces from the auditorium platforms of their particular schools; as they stare out at us from the printed pages of our newspapers, reminding us of the swiftness of the years, for you will join that throng of seniors all too soon. Thus, today, I must write of your mentors.

"Mentors," Child, so that you do not have to look up the term in your dictionary, means those who have influenced or directed your path from this, the springtime of your life, into that tomorrow when you will ascend the graduating platform. The mentors have been many, Child. They include your teachers from your Sunday school years (I may have first told you of Christ and His great love for you, but they kept you reminded of Him and of your task in letting others know of that love); your Girl's Auxiliary leader (I may have made an effort at teaching you the symbolism in the purity of white, the sincerity of gold and that of green for growth, but she reminded you of it at your weekly meetings, lest in forgetting you would become less a lady).

Then of course there have been your teachers in your schools. If you were a boy, there would be your coach as well, who played his greatest game in developing your integrity for fair play and honest evaluation of your fellowmen; but you are a girl. Your teachers had moral values in mind when they subtly and tactfully led you into the ways of womanhood as they imparted to you intellectual truths.

Your mentors, Child, include all of those who have instilled these good things into your life. I, with you, will be even more aware of them on that tomorrow when your eyes meet my own across the footlights of the graduate's stage—those who were able to implant into your total being the awareness that "knowledge comes, but wisdom remains."

There is something amiss in trekking to the mailbox at midnight. I'm not exactly sure what it is, but in my rural environment, there is something not right about it. Possibly it is the fact that all the world sleeps around me—the whippoorwills, the tree frogs, the katydids, even the bullfrogs in the pasture pond are quiet—as I go marching out to the mailbox for the evening paper that no one has picked up. But I'm a late retirer. Early retirers and heavy sleepers miss a lot, I always say, and a part of my daily activities is reading the evening newspaper. So if company is around or if we have spent the evening away from home and the paper is still in the mailbox, I just can't leave it there—instead, I find myself trailing across the front lawn that is wet with dew to gather in the evening tidbits.

By midnight, of course, the spiders have made their webs from shrub to shrub, and I instinctively put my hand across my face to shield it from the silvery threads that I know await me in the darkness. The grass is soft and slippery beneath my house shoes. The night air is heavy in the lunar stillness, creating a foggy mist that hangs in the treetops and across the lighted windows, making dim the streaks of light across the grass as I trudge back toward the house.

Jack the collie looks up from his favorite forbidden sleeping spot—the flower planter. He is too drowsy to jump up quickly at my appearance as he usually does when caught at the act during the daylight hours. I let him alone; he's too peaceful there.

I sniff the fragrant aroma of the honeysuckle as the night lies quiet about me. Nothing is stirring in the stillness except for the Angus across the pasture fence where there in the moonlight they are rhythmically nipping away the tender blades of grass, filling their stomachs in the cool night so that tomorrow they can lie in the shade when the sun beams down brightly. They raise their heads to look at me, probably questioning my own nighttime hours, wondering, no doubt, if I am as confused as they.

They return to their business at hand, and I enter my front door, closing out the quiet night. Feeling like an alien, I sit down with my newspaper, conscious of my incongruency to the nocturnal world. And then suddenly it hits me! I know what is wrong—I'm reading yesterday's news! Trailing along as usual, behind in my efforts to keep abreast of life itself. But not God's creatures of nature; they know the proper time for waking—set in motion by the Clockmaker himself.

Summer

Dear August:

I wanted to write to you, August, because like all other time, you will be gone before I have had a chance to tell you how I feel about you, or that I have enjoyed your presence—but I have. I have loved your lazy, pink mornings as the sun started to climb upward, making its debut just as I was preparing my family's breakfast. That was during my second hour; my first hour in the morning is devoted to my typewriter, while my family sleeps.

I've especially enjoyed that first hour of each of your days, August. The quietness that you offered. The damp softness of your grass on our lawn when I wanted to stretch my legs and strengthen my imagination somewhat as I traipsed around outside, breathing deeply of the fresh country air just before the break of a new day. I shared a communion with the whole world it seemed, as my own little part of it lay hushed around me. I even shared a fellowship with the shepherd and the spitz, who are usually quite loud-mouthed and always bark at our emergence from the indoors each morning, for even they remained quiet when I would slip surreptitiously outside to sit on the back step in the early morning darkness.

They would saunter close to me, as though wanting to be a part of my intrinsic thoughts, and often I sat there on the steps, with the dogs lying close to me, as I watched the dawn. It is like the breaking of spring—one moment a gray heaviness encircles the earth, the next moment, a fresh new day. In its dawning there is a message for humanity, like a sorrow that bears an indescribable weight on the soul, then lifts so that burdens become bearable.

Thus, watching for the lovely patterns in nature—the arrival of dawn—I forget the troublesome patterns of the changing life styles in our culture. I am saddened, somewhat, that the atrocities in the one overlap the beauties in the other.

But August, forgive me, I got carried away; back to your lovely world. I've loved the early chirping of our mocking-bird that feels as much at home here as I do, holding an al-most twenty-four hour vigil on behalf of his young, with our own young ones charged a five-cent penalty payment for every one of his species that a BB happens to clip off the fence by mistake.

I don't know why we apply the term *him* to our mocking-bird, for aside from grammatical error, there are many of his species around here, of both the masculine and the feminine gender. When we talk of the mockingbird, he is special, as though he has had no descendants over the period of years that we have lived here. In April, he perches in our tall wal-nut tree in the front yard, and I hear him singing his heart out during our morning breakfast hour. In summer, he moves to our orchard trees, where he and his mate can be seen flit-ting about low on the ground, trying to divert the shepherd's attention to some area other than the orchard, for evidently they have a young family there and the huge, shaggy dog rep-resents a threat to them as he moves about in the grass beneath the trees. Then, in the fall, our mockingbird is back again on the television antenna, once more singing his happy song.

I've loved the proud look on our Spot's face, August, as

she comes tripping through the orchard just after dawn each morning with bounty for her young—horrible looking field mice. Her young lunge for her offering, taking the dangling dark creatures in their own teeth, arching their backs against their mother with a "Gee, Mom, you're swell" gesture.

Kittens, too, know when they are loved and wanted, especially when their sire is mindful of their needs as well, for there, high on a limb in the backyard yawns our big yellow- and white-streaked Sunglow, exercising his feline masculine authority by curling up in a favorite maple tree. He stares into my window each morning as I open the blinds, and I vow he could be correctly termed a Peeping Tom! Why else would he have chosen the limb just outside my bedroom as his nightly perch?

Soon now, August, your leaves will turn to a faded yellow and your grass a pale brown. The katydids will quiet down and the bobwhite's serenade will cease. A chill will hover over the earth, following your warm summer evenings. You will be gone, leaving fall in your stead. I have loved you, as I have filled jar after jar of jelly from your abundant berry supply and walked through my vegetable garden heavy with proof of your offering—beans, tomatoes, young peppers, and corn. There's the new garden that we will plant during your latter days, its harvest coming to us in late autumn, when I will need a jacket to gather in the vegetables before the first frost, storing them in the basement for days following.

Your gifts from our orchard have been wonderful, too, August: apples, brilliant red and golden yellow; pears, hanging in heavy clusters; grapes, luscious and fragrant, and wasting in their abundance. I have loved the heavy "expectancy" that you bring to our Holsteins, August, as nature prepares them for their fall freshening, for that is the crucial new beginning for dairy herds—a fresh flourish of milk to feed the millions who wait upon their own offering.

Oh, yes, August, one other thing! The wardrobe for my

household! I've barely got their spring one paid for, and here you remind me that it is time for a new one—fall clothes, back-to-school clothes for the children, and a new uplifting coat of paint for our farm buildings—before the winter season gets too near at hand.

Ah, August, where has your time gone? And my time gone? Am I the only one around here who worries about time? Just like at the pool the other day on the children's last swim for this year. (One can learn a lot about people in the swimming pool.) As I watched, anxious mothers chased after their young, afraid to let them try their wings; perfunctory parents enjoyed their own pleasures while their young went too far out; rambunctious youths, happy with the water's depth, were unmindful of its harm; languid lifeguards, complacent in the pool's no-casualty summer record, dozed lazily on their perches in the sun. I watched them, August, conscious of the hot afternoon wind that blew with a nostalgic hint of time flown in its breath, as though whispering to the carefree summer people: I won't come your way again. This is my final passing.

I found myself wanting to cry out to them, August. I wanted to say to them: How right is that echo in the wind! How like time it flees, but to where? Hang onto it, don't let it go—there is something so utterly indescribable about its passing. Someday, August, I may be better able to describe passing time—but this day I could not. I could only think of Shakespeare who, like I, worried about time's unending quest to destroy, and of Job, who, in that dearest of books, said of his own life: "My days are swifter than a weaver's shuttle...."

None of the others there at the pool seemed aware of the "swift-footed thief" silently stealing away this season, this succulent young day—none but the dry summer wind and me.

But, August, if you are symbolic of passing time, almost mocking us with your magnificent gifts to the land while we stand so idly by, curious as to what we've given with another year of our own lives, you, even so, bring to us another gift to be enjoyed with each additional year's passing—the gift of memories. Each year in August they will be remembered—vivid anecdotes that were shared with my young in the summertime of their youth. Some, even, of the swimming pool itself, for my young were not always so proficient in the bright blue waves, and I recall numerous other days that I sat by the pool, waiting.

As a matter of fact, for two weeks out of three consecutive summers I sat by the pool in the hot summer sun and watched as my young absorbed the instructions of their directors, who patiently taught them swimming and lifesaving. The process of watching was painful at times because all the other kids seemed to outdo my own. I sat, hopeful with parental pride beaming from my sunburned brow, as our eldest would stride across the breadth of the diving board calling, "Hey, Mom! Watch this!" sure that he was headed for a cool graceful plunge into the water's depth as those students ahead of him were doing, only to have his aspirations fizzle out as he stared into the abyss of swirling waves at his feet. Then, his long skinny legs would drop slowly, almost softly down into the pool while his scrawny little arms clung to the diving board as long as possible.

Sometimes Dad would take a turn driving the youngsters in for their swimming lessons and sometimes he would merely accompany all of us, but he would squirm on his seat at the above antics and turn a little red in the face when I would call out to the "Hey, Mom," salutes with my own, "Oh, yes, that's fine."

After three years of such endeavors, I went again with my youngsters and a young visitor to a neighbor's pool that had been constructed as a place for the neighborhood youth to swim. The pool was complete with diving board, but minus a lifeguard. My own, finally benefiting from their swimming lessons, were well out into the depth of the pool, and I had instructed the younger child to stay near the edge, feeling sure that she had understood the dividing area separating the shallow water from the deep. I settled down with my newspaper at the pool's edge, and when I looked up again I felt a sickening nausea in my stomach. Only two heads were visible on the water's surface—those of my own two children in the center of the pool! Then I saw the black hair spreading out in long dark tresses as it bobbed up and down toward the surface of the clear blue water.

I screamed to my own youngsters. Instantly, the brown arms of our eldest flashed across the surface of the pool in the gleaming sunlight. I no longer heard the "Hey, Mom, watch this!" But instead, I heard gentle, reassuring tones directed to the frightened child: "It's okay, I've got you," as he brought the slender little figure to the water's edge, and to safety.

And to think, I was the only spectator. The memory will always be mine, in August.

Less dramatic memories of quieter "homedays" that my children treasured in their very early years hopefully will continue into their adult days. Homedays, those days when windows were open to the summer sun and the screeching of our front porch swing could be heard as young legs pushed it to and fro, barely touching the floor with first one foot and then the other in a strenuous effort to keep the swing moving. Suddenly the sound would stop, and I would hear: "Hey, Mom! Can you come out for a talk?"

Sometimes eagerly, sometimes reluctantly, but I hope never impatiently, I would turn the boiling jelly-kettle off, and with coffee in one hand and something cold for my young one in the other, I would make my way outside for a "talk."

So we talked, and now, remembering, I have the treasure

and they perhaps have no recollection of what transpired in the afternoons when we had our talks in the summer time.

Other memories come, of not too peaceful days—of children's fusses and the "me first" terms that drifted through my open kitchen window.

"Boy! Have you got a lot to learn! You know company always comes first . . . " our eldest was complaining to his sister on one such day. Other children's voices drifted in to me from the outside, and I knew that any moment I would hear the familiar "Hey, Mom, make . . . " as the conversation continued on our front lawn.

If I didn't intervene, it wasn't because I didn't want to teach my youngest politeness; it was because I wanted her to develop her own initiative for that which she had already been taught, and I recalled such a day when she was five. We had been having a bit of trouble where "sharing" was concerned, especially when there was only one thing to share. But we had been working at the problem. I wasn't sure, however, how much progress had been made in the right direction until one hot summer day when my young daughter "didn't have anyone to play with." So out of a busy day of preparing food from our garden for the freezer, I took time to have lunch with her in her playhouse.

Anticipating my visit at lunch time, she had prepared raw cucumbers with a white sauce of flour and water poured over them, and cut up squash—too tough for the freezer—and of course, the usual mud pies. Beside my plate she had properly placed her only old fork, knife, and spoon. Beside her plate, there was nothing at all. I opened my mouth to protest, intending to offer some extra pieces of my own silverware for this special occasion. But just then she said, "Mommie, will you say the blessing?"

So sitting there at the playhouse table, while my daughter sat across from me with a look about her which plainly said that insofar as she was concerned, this day she was entertaining royalty, I bowed my head and thanked God for our food. Then I picked up my fork and pretended to eat the raw vegetables as I told her what a fine cook that she was and asked for a recipe. In queenly dignity, she pretended to eat, too, as though she had a fork in her hand. Blinking a tear or two away from my eyes, I never pretended that she didn't.

I could not remember the summer time without recalling Rocky, August, with his sensitive brown eyes, so exemplary of his shepherd breed, staring out to us from his dark face that tied directly in line with his brown legs and feet.

When the weather was nice, I did not see much of Rocky, except to see him trailing at a distance behind the youngsters' bikes or with them and Princess the pony. Wherever they were playing, Rocky was not far away. In the afternoons I would see him making his journey across the pasture beside my husband as they brought the Holsteins home. He waited eagerly each afternoon for just the slightest signal to push the cows along homeward—which he was not allowed to do unless bidden.

I did not always find him on the carport during the day in summer, either, for he was just as likely to be down the road on Grandma's front porch, where he visited with her Skippy. They roamed, too, for miles around but when the clouds rolled up in dark streaks across the sky, and the thunder started to roar, our Rocky would head for home and his family.

We accepted his nervousness at stormy weather because we understood his problem: he was singed a bit by lightning when he was a very young fellow, and he had come rushing home to us. After that day, we allowed him his place on the back porch utility. In fact. we came to observe his actions as our weather guide; if he stopped and lay down at the entrance, his conduct told us that the thunderstorm would be a mild one. If he went farther and crawled under the utility table, we knew to expect lightning. If he got up from that location and moved on into the den with us, we started peering out windows and wondering whether to go into the storm cellar.

I associate Rocky with my writing because often, as I have been inside my study deep in thought, with no one in our big house except me, I would hear a gentle tapping at the back door. I would recognize the sound even before I heard the thunder, and I would leave my work and go to the back door to answer his knock, for his gentle, persistent tapping could scarcely go unheard.

As summer fades away and early fall days are near, a new exuberance for life seems to awaken within our breasts. We greet the days more eagerly, and in spite of ourselves, ready for that new season ahead.

This year, August, I am remembering the words of an acquaintance regarding your presence as she stated: "The days are so nice now. I just look forward to waking each morning. Late summer and early fall days just seem to make our troubles lighter." Certainly, most of the people in our society do have problems, for few people escape worries of some nature. Some of them carry their burdens aloft, like the leaves in early spring, turned upward and outward—filled with sap and stigma, never falling to touch the earth below. Others are like the fall foliage, August—they sag and sway, and finally wilt to the waiting bosom of earth where strength lies.

If then, August, your late summer days can lift the heart, perhaps that is another reason that I have loved you.

Fall

Ah, September, and a moment of tranquility in my back yard.
I hang the sheets to dry and observe the trees in our back pasture, their leaves blotched now in rustiness by the coming fall
season. The lawn is strewn with fallen brown leaves that de-
mand the attention of my yard broom. I ignore them, except
for the rustle made by Tippy the spitz as he trudges toward
the lawn chair, seeking me out just as I am about to seclude
myself with pen and writing pad, away from the morning
noises of washing machine and vacuum cleaner.

Here, all is quiet, barring those distinct sounds of nature
that accompany an early fall day in the country—the constant
murmurings of little creatures in the trees, part chirp, part
hum, echoing continuously all morning high above my head
in the cottonwood and maples. In the distance behind me toward the wood-covered hill, a woodpecker taps out a tune,
and in the valley beyond the knoll I hear a neighbor's hammer,
gently tapping away at a stone structure that will outlast him.
In the spacious blueness the gentle coo of the turtledove re-
sounds, its treble encircling the countryside.

I lie back in my chair and close my eyes, enjoying this quiet
moment, this solitude, and I am thankful for the moment,

for the quietness of home, and for the joy of listening. There is something inexpressible about nature's peaceful sounds. To those of us who value nature as God's gift to us, it "speaks a various language."

I have treasured moments spent with my young when we shared together the quiet joy of listening. Though I could teach them of the beauty in nature, I could not impart to them the abstract loveliness that I felt for it; this they would have to find within themselves. Then one day, our eldest, cocking an ear toward the sound of our mockingbird singing high on the television antenna, had said to me, "Listen to him, Mom! Hear him?" Then I knew that my son and I shared a common value, whether initiated at my own instruction or from that greater mentor—the land.

Soon now, September's faded greens will change to October's red and yellows, with orange- and purple-streaked sunrises offering promise and hope for each new day. Before October makes her exit, she must turn her mauve blanketed sunsets to banks of winter gray, setting the stage for the wild geese to make their seasonal pilgrimage across billowy skies; before her reign is finished, her crystalline coating of white will hover over the land, as she finishes her magic spell on the world in crispy decay. Then the homemakers will pile high October's offering—golden beautiful leaves—burning them to a charred nothingness, as though clearing away the proof that she were here at all.

I consider the falling leaves of our walnut tree which starts to shed in September, each alternate year showing forth its heavy array of fruit. As the leaves, in their sparseness, reveal the tree's huge black walnuts, my thoughts begin: so, I tell myself, is life—for how many stages and phases must we go through during our span of years, shedding each in its turn, before the real fruit of a life is borne? How many summers, like the one going out? How many winters, as the one coming in? How much preparation for the final curtain, until we have given our life to humanity, whether or not it was good or bad?

This favorite tree, planted by Grandma when she was a young lady, has weathered many of nature's storms with only its limbs damaged at times. It has taught me many lessons as I have observed it year after year. We have cut its top back a few times, but it has not been hampered for long by such trivial cunning of man's art; its trunk only served to become stronger and more firmly anchored in the earth.

It has offered a shade for the neighborhood pea-shellings and apple-peelings in days long past, in that earlier agrarian culture in which neighbors got together for such functions. It was not impeded by nails driven into its straight body, but the thick rough bark grew right back, covering its wounds. It offered a place for summer Sunday "visiting," where old men whittled and young men wheedled, before the days of air-conditioning.

Now, there on our lawn, it offers a cool shade all summer for our mockingbird and bluejay, and in winter, a nestling place for the starlings that line its barren limbs from tip end to trunk.

Back again to October, for I must write of her artistic decor as she blends her shades of browns and golds and reds, of the rustle of her leaves beneath my feet as I have walked with my youngsters in our world of togetherness, for I learned early in my maternal role that nothing could bring the intrinsic depth of youth to its surface as could a peaceful walk in God's infinite universe; so have we walked in mid-October on a wood-covered hillside. I would pause amid the carpet of brown autumn leaves and listen. There would be no sound, except for the louder rustle of leaves made by the shepherd as he pushed along in the distance. I would gaze wonderingly at the picturesque scene—the remaining yellow and red leaves on the trees as they sloped downward on the hillside, encircling the valley below blanketed in goldenrod. I would stand there in awe of nature, the wondrous decorator, admiring the simple taste and the blending of the color shades.

Then, ahead, I would hear, as my presence was missed—

"Let's wait on Mom. She's tired." So my young ones would stop to wait until I caught up with them, and my interlude with nature would be broken, for they refused to believe that I was not lonely as I stood there amid the trees.

Perhaps in time, they too will make the discovery that our Creator is very near at hand among the wonders of His creation, which was the purpose of the walk, really, as together we discovered the world about us: the hole here was made by a groundhog, that one up there in the tree by a squirrel, already filled, no doubt, with nuts for the winter ahead. I would take a small hand in each of my own as we walked together and talked of the little things that we saw, for I knew that if we walked together often enough I could tell them someday of the bigger things—of the reason for my not being alone as I stood there among the trees on the hill.

Even though the land and the rural world has been a part of my children's past, it may not be a part of their future. Perhaps by choice; more awesome, by compulsion, as the population continues to increase and expanding cities that are like crawling, creeping fingers reach out across the land, their suburbs greedily grasping up golden daffodils and green meadows that poets write about.

Thus, as our society is preparing itself for the decay of the rural world, I, too, must prepare my own children for their juxtaposition with the urban. But in the preparation for their transition from the rustic, rural world of their youth to the more society-oriented suburban world of their tomorrow, they must not forget the land. From our soil, that may one day stand in concrete, they must receive a legacy: they must remember the strength it has given, the hope it has implanted in anxious hearts with its shoots of new life in the spring; the fulfillment it has offered in autumn with heavy harvest borne; the peace from its hills from "whence cometh our help" in all seasons, whether in pictorial October, seeping with the lushness of life in spring, or blanketed in snow in winter.

So, we walked in October, and as we walked, we talked, reluctantly, almost, of that tomorrow that might be theirs. We spoke of the day of artificial milk, ominously threatening our Walnut Hill already; the day of artificial food, when a few plants may provide that which it has taken acres to produce heretofore in man's struggle for his place on the land; or even the day of artificial life. The thought seemed too awesome for even expectant youth, perhaps for the adult layman as well, but not for the scientist, who must ever press forward in the study of man and his resources in an endless search of a better tomorrow, in the process succinctly crushing our way of life with his every discovery.

Surely then, we must pause in October to observe the ties with the land that bring a richness to life, such as the stableness of the changing seasons, the insistence of the universe that God is in His heaven yet, that all is well.

And now, November—

The drone of a plane overhead awoke me. The fall night is quiet about me as the plane passes on. It left no bombs, brought no disasters. This is America, land of freedom and opportunity.

I slide out of bed, get into my house slippers and steal silently toward the front of the house so that I do not wake my sleeping family. The moonlight from a lovely autumn night floods my living room and I stand for a moment, peering out into the night, enjoying its stillness.

Outside, the fields lie hushed and barren for the most part, where the farmer has reaped his bounties—they have been good this year—for once more the earth has brought forth an abundant harvest. Family members across the miles prepare to make their journey homeward to spend Thanksgiving, and it is a good season that approaches—and a good season that has already been. There have been so many blessings of food and provisions that have lasted us another year, causing us to feel a kinship with our early American forefathers as they gathered to offer praise for their tangible bounties. We, too, offer praise for our own at this season—praise perhaps not spoken, but communicated, through gratitude for the glorious season around us.

Chattering blackbirds fill the crispy brown treetops in our back pasture, and just stepping out-of-doors brings a lilt to my heart as I stand and listen to the happy chorus. Such off-key chirping from the carefree life of the gregarious bird world has disillusioned our mockingbird no doubt, for he sits sulkily on the telephone wire, his happy summer song gone. The starling, with its clear cry, has moved in to take the mockingbird's place.

The glossy black and white speckled older starlings and the light brown younger starlings line the limbs of the huge cottonwood just outside my study window. The branches, stripped now of their broad green leaves with only noisy clusters of seed-pods remaining, make a thumping sound as the fall wind whips them against the gutter. Come spring, though, the starling will have fled and our mockingbird will be back there, singing his heart out as he peers in over my shoulder. It has been a good season for the birds, too, and they are busy now in the brown harvested fields gathering up wasted grain. They are thankful, I imagine, for the as-yet-imperfected harvesting machines that leave a little and spill a little as they go about their business.

As lovely azure days give way to shimmering cloudy ones, and crispy, frosty mornings bow in retreat to damp December, the only other thing that I can think to add about you, November, is that you will not pass my way again—not you, not the same November.

Winter

Today I must write of winter, of the quiet whiteness that blankets our pastures, of the loud shrill whistle of the starling as he looks for grain scraps behind the dairy barn, sounding almost human in his frantic search for food that the snow has covered. I must write of my busy farmer husband, as I look across our back pasture and see him bringing home a mother cow and her new baby calf through the heavy falling snow, holding the tiny bovine form close to his chest, offering human warmth to the small stiff body—nature knows no season for completing her work. Thus, I must write of things this day, of snow and dead of winter.

As long as the electricity keeps coming in, we can make it. However, when the electric current stops, as has happened in the past and no doubt will happen yet before the winter is over, then I have a unique subject—of farm lives accustomed to modern today's world trying to function with the inconveniences of yesterday's world, with kerosene lanterns for barn chores and kerosene lamps for indoors, and meals cooked on the living room fireplace—provided of course that fire logs happen to be on hand. Inside our farm home, with the television off, there is a warm coziness that families used to know, with entertainment coming from games, or even better, conversation, corn popping over the open fire, potatoes baking on the smoldering coals, and snow cream made from the freshly fallen snow on the lawn and sweet cream from the dairy.

As yet, we still have the current, in spite of the heavy snowstorm during the night, even though the trees and shrubbery droop and sway with their weight of ice. Fences stand twice their natural size with transparent icicles hanging from them. A lone crow flies overhead, looking for a place to set his own weight down, but finding no such place, flies on.

No tracks are visible in the snow except for those of the shepherd and Miss Kitty, and those of brave red chanticleer who dared to leave the cluster of warm fowl about him in his chickenhouse environs and step warily toward his watering pan, lifting his yellow webbed feet high with each cautious step.

My young, upon awaking, see the snow outside and clamor for the out-of-doors, and out come caps and boots and heavy pants from the closet shelves.

I stand at my kitchen window and watch as they romp up and down in the path that their dad has shoveled out, piling the snow by shovelfuls on either side of the path until it looks like a narrow roadway cut into a white hill. The shepherd hears their happy shouts and bounds toward them. Miss Kitty hears them, too, and joins in the parade. They make a picturesque foursome as they frolic there, the boy and the girl, the dog and the cat. I can resist the urge no longer, so I join them there, and together we start to roll up huge balls of snow, fashioning them into a saucy-looking fellow with a tall black top hat and a black button nose.

The snow is clean and crystal white about us, no stains of pollution mar its beauty—not yet. The air is crisp and penetrating, filling our lungs with gulps of pure freshness. The world lies peacefully still around us, except for an occasional snap of breaking limbs that may be heard from the forest on the back hillside, as the ice breaks down the heavy limbs.

As the trees stand dormant and barren, stripped of their green cloaks, one is better able to see their true uniqueness, their individualities: the large, strong oaks that have stood for years, towering over the tender young hickories; the sweet-gum, knarry and rough from the oozing sticky gum escaping its bark; the willow, bent and depressed.

I observe the outstretched branches that are personified representations suggesting to me the world of humans; for just as God made the unique trees, so He made men. To some have been assigned great tasks, like the towering trees of the forest; but most of us are more truly represented by the smaller trees—the struggling, weaker trees—who have less to contribute with our lives, except for that superb element that undergirds the network of humanity—support. And when we have found our rightful place, our own little niche, then, like the supporting trees of the forest, we have found our place of service.

So December moves on, and it is my season to write of peace on earth, good will toward men—of Christmas time, unity and family love. It is my time to describe the eager look on the faces of the young as they anticipate a visit from Santa; to tell of the cherubic faces of the very young, as they behold for the first time in their lives the lighted tree, the star; or to tell of older, tired faces, those filled with pain, observing the blinking Christmas ornaments for the last Christmas season of their lives. A sad season, a joyful season; and at our house Dad takes the chopping axe across his shoulder and, with our eldest at his side, the two of them set out toward the pasture pond to bring home a Christmas tree; the man, with long and even strides, pausing now and then to wait on the young one at times beside him and at times behind him, kicking at the snow with a red rubber boot; stooping to pick up tiny handfuls of snow, tossing it high into the air and then laughing gaily as the misty flakes sift back across his flushed face.

Soon now the house will smell of pine needles and cedar and spices and ham, clearly establishing once again the season that is upon us, the time to gather in memories that will be garnered again, like so many memories, when our young have left this house. Memories of Christmases and of Christmas Eves when I have been so perturbed with Mrs. Santa for allowing her poor husband to leave the North Pole without helping him assemble his bag full of toys first! The major part of Christmas Eve nights were spent in the living room, inserting hex nuts and bolts and screws into tricycles and bicycles and wagons. At least I have learned what "hex" nuts are, so the experience was not wasted, for I consider all experiences valuable in one way or another.

Then, after all the screws were finally inserted and all the cardboard boxes shaken and the clutter cleared away, I would stand back and look, surer than ever that Santa was becoming less wise with every Christmas season, for he continued to leave things at our house that were forever taking up extra space, like a doll's huge feeding chair for the kitchen, taking up as much room at the kitchen table as an ordinary kitchen chair or a tiny doll bathinette replacing the area used for the bathroom heater. Beside a youth bed, a doll bed found its way, only to be moved back and forth each evening when I bent low to tuck in a tiny "Mommie" at bedtime.

But then, small faces would glisten with happiness; a firm young hand would hold tenaciously to my own as we walked together: "Mom, I think the best Christmas present of all is that we love each other, and God." Soft lips would reach up to kiss my cheek, "Gee, Mom, this is the nicest ever. . . . " Then I would reevaluate Mr. and Mrs. Santa. Maybe they were not quite so foolish, after all.

And now, Christmases have come and gone, and our young are growing up. But the occasion is still observed at our house and the season is once again upon us. Time once more for the family gift exchange with grandparents and uncles and aunts. I'm not sure when the custom of observing Christmas Eve and a family gift exchange at our house began, but years ago, when there were fewer of us; when there were only nieces and nephews, before there were precious grandnieces.

As the years have passed, we have lost some of those dear faces that were so traditionally a part of Christmas for so many years—smiles that will never be forgotten, memories that so vividly accompany Christmas Eves of the past. But we have gained some faces, too, a special tiny face this year, with features so very like those of that dear face gone from us. As I sit among torn Christmas wrappings, too weary to restore order to the living room tonight, the realization comes to me that this is the way it is with families—those whom we give up are not really gone, but a part of them lives on to renew life, and in such, memories, with each new season.

Now the fireplace claims my attention, and I am reminded that Santa will not make a journey down the sooty chimney tonight, for our young have grown past the stage of expecting his appearance from such direction. Thus the bearded old fellow is taking a respite at our house, but he will come again, with his bag of little trucks and tiny toy tractors, and dolls and doll houses. And I? If I am not here then, I will be just a memory away on Christmas Eve, encircling the shadows, the flickering fire flames, the dying embers on the hearth. And that other part of me will have joined the missing face from our family circle. But we will be remembered, and loved, if I, too, have left a grandchild in my corner.

I recall my grandmother's home at Christmas time, and the huge table that she always had set up from corner to corner, set at an angle across her huge kitchen, so that all of us could eat at the same table, the old and the young alike. No parking the young off at a separate table while the adults visited; we all ate at the large table, and we minded our manners, too, if we had any; and most of us did if we ate near my grandfather, who thought nothing of reaching under the white table cloth and quietly pinching the grandchild that was getting too loud or behaving in any manner that he deemed inappropriate to the occasion.

It was a gay and happy time, and all of us, the older ones as well as the youngsters, looked forward to the hour after the dinner dishes were finished when we had the "Christmas tree."

I remember my grandfather's straight oak chair by the window that he tilted back and leaned against the wall. There he would wait patiently, with one eye squinched slightly above the other—and I was a grown young lady before I learned that he could only see from one of them—as he waited for his gifts to be placed on the floor beside him before he started to open any of his packages. His gray mustache, the exact color of his receding gray hair that curled slightly over each ear, reached almost to his shirt collar, and would twitch upward, toward one side, as his pile of gifts continued to mount.

He enjoyed the occasion, sitting there with a tender smile on his face as he waited for all of us to open our gifts before he tackled his own. Then, after all our gifts were opened, we all took turns opening his and my grandmother's brightly wrapped packages, reiterating to each of them whom the gift was from, for we were always a bit impatient at their slowness in untying the ribbons.

It was a good feeling of warmth and love that we experienced at my grandmother's house on Christmas Day. There was the knowledge, too, that there had been sacrifice in the giving, and because of it, the meaning of Christmas stood forthwith.

I do not know many families today that are held together

by love as was my grandmother's household, and as long as she lived most of us returned again to her house on Christmas Day. Even in her eighties, she still maintained her Christmas tree, her wrapped gifts, and her love for each of us.

There is just something about the after-mighnight hours that attract the writer, especially the white winter after-midnight hours. And wasn't it Plato who said that a work is "spoilt" when not done at the right time. Thus, the writing on this February night as snow glistens outside my study window when I turn out my inside light so that I can glimpse a more vivid view of the wintry world. The dark shadows of the huge cottonwood stretch themselves across the white snow beneath my window. The trimmed hedgerow, anxious to start the spring growth so nearly within its grasp now, makes a dark outline across the back lawn.

Inside my study, the red glow from the electric heater flashes on and off in the darkness, and I sit quietly, absorbing the alabaster beauty of the gently sloping hills beneath brilliant stars. How magnificent our universe. How marvelous, and how mystical that I cannot distinguish the stars in the heavens from man, who seems to weave in and out among them in his flying machine with its flickering bright lights. Yet, to man who journeys there tonight, the stars seem just as far removed as they do to me in my darkened study.

How magnificent the universe; how almost unbelievable, too, that on that brilliant moon in the sky there exists hills and valleys. How ridiculous, almost, that mankind should climb the hills on that bright vessel that lights this earth so beautifully, when there are so many mountains here that have not yet been surmounted.

How magnificent the universe, and how peaceful, especially the white February nights in rural America. The ecologists tell us that we only have a few years more of this tranquility unless man gets his mind on his business and removes from his environment some of the debris that progress has brought. If he doesn't, then our beauty will be turned into ugliness.

Ah, quiet night. I know that you are passing too swiftly, that tomorrow is church day; but tomorrow belongs to the wife and mother, and tonight's quiet beauty belongs to the writer and muse, and to the environs of the study where I have written my thoughts down as the years have gone by— sometimes late at night, sometimes early in the day, often on joyful occasions, when my heart was elated with the blessings that I have received from the land, from my family, from friends, and surely from the hand of God.

But tonight I sit absorbed in my thoughts, stunned, almost, to the point of numbness as I look out on that quiet world, questioning the turmoil within my soul. . . . I live again the painful recent experience as it became apparent to us that change was upon our household. As the hand of fate, if you will, reached out ever so gently at first and touched our lives. Then more ferociously it knocked.

"What's the matter, Dad?. . . Something wrong with your hands, Dad?" the children questioned at first. "What's wrong with your legs, Dad? You need help? Why can't you stand up, Dad?"

And the straight figure who bore the burden of our family mortgage stooped and started to limp. Brawny hands, overnight it seemed, were weakened in strength to that of a child's hands. Healthy knees suddenly rendered themselves indequate to bear the weight which they had borne for a mere forty-eight years as the great crippler, rheumatoid arthritis, cast its shadow over the most wonderful place in the world to us— home.

I went again and looked at the rose vine, the one I wrote about at the beginning of this book, and I knew that I had distorted its acquiescence to its fate on the day it was pruned, for surely it did flinch when the shears were applied. If I had looked more carefully, I would have discovered that the vine wept for days after the pruning had been completed as tiny drops of moisture trickled from its wounded stem. Had I observed the stem more closely, I would have realized that the deep wound did not heal smoothly but that its new covering grew in darker fashion, reflecting warped edges as if from pain, though perhaps thicker now, and more strong in depth.

When the doctors said, regarding my husband's condition, "We don't know why these things happen, whether they are from heredity, the results of the environment, or the act of God—all that we can be sure of in our profession is that we take what is left and do the best we can with it," then I knew I was back again to my plant, the one that I had so often epitomized as stunted in its growth by the tumult of flood and wind and hail, but in spite of all the fierce forces of nature the plant struggled and stood stalwart, and grew and produced its harvest. Now I knew that the plant required more essentials for its survival than I had ever realized. More nutrients than fertilizer and damp earth were needed, for if it were to lift its head among the others in its milieu then surely it must neglect to reveal the deep fear menacing its rising up each day—the ominous threat that one day it will not rise up at all, and its leaves will not fill out as the sun descends upon them, but that they will remain folded and twisted, like blades of grass waiting for the summer rain.

Surely, then, the plant receives its strength by communicating with something more magnanimous than itself. And I, in my minuteness, stand amazed at the tremendous weight on the shoots of life encumbered by the earth's crust.

And now, on this February day, the white dairy barn is strangely quiet. The milking machine pulsators that greeted the dawn in the still falling snow on a winter day, or in the mist of an early August morning, are hushed. The Holsteins have been loaded on to trucks and hauled away, with all of us, including Jack the collie peering after them as far as our eyes could see. They leave their muddy hoofprints in the barnyard lot, their silage feeding areas, and hay, strewn yet in the hayracks, with its crispy, clover smell; and their memories, of a way of life that can only be remembered as good.

I stand at my kitchen window, the same window through which I have observed some of the scenes in this book, and today I observe the cold, yellowish crackling world of winter. The pale grass, the curling leaves of the shrubbery coiled back by the bitter winds; the hedgerow, bending and lifting; the barren tree limbs, swaying and rising up again. Standing here, I feel a strong association with these natural objects of my environment; a sentiment that "bend we may, but break we shan't" because our foothold is here, coddled in the blanket that is earth, and like the process of osmosis almost, we absorb at the right time—whether or not we are aware of it— what we need to sustain us through periods of dormancy and depression. This footing we share makes me know that there is a warmer day, a spring day, when burdens will be lighter— a day when blades of new grass will appear that were not here before.

Thus, the strength that the earth gives to me becomes an abstract entity almost, hanging there just inside my kitchen window and beyond it, to lift, to comfort, to encircle me in the folds of warmth on even this February day.

Spring Again

Thank you, Lord, for these quiet moments. I have so few of them now. Thank you for whatever time, hours or moments, that You see fit to allow me when there is no one else around except the two of us. Together we observe the greenness of spring, the yellow of the forsythia, the lush shades of the tulip, and the pale elegance of the late jonquil. All of mankind cannot behold with you these joys, for some of them are not blessed with this precious gift of sight.

Thank you for the melodious tones of sound—the song of birds, the hum of bees, the distant purring of the tractor across the hill from our back pasture—for it is spring again, when man once more starts to turn up the soil, seeking a livelihood from its depth. I can appreciate more the sound, Lord, because I know the sensations with which man sets about his task. I, too, feel a unison with the land, a tie that is not forgotten, no matter how busy or humdrum my life may become.

Thank you for the beautiful smell of springtime, for the aura of growing things, for the redolent breath of peach blossoms, of the hyacinth, the rose. Thank you, Lord, especially thank you for the rose, for it guides me into an even deeper relationship with the land. I can appreciate the prickly, biting touch of its hard-working stem, striving ever to pull itself upward toward a better life and its more delicate touch, the soft velvety feel of its blossom, for in its touch I am taught, Lord; taught to appreciate the perfection of your handiwork: the entwinement of the bitter with the sweet, the gentle with the sharp, and the rough with the smooth. In such knowledge I can better understand your other creations—the vivid feel of a child's soft skin, reminding me that all things young are beautiful: a newborn infant, a growing child, firm and round and romping, or the weathered touch of the aged and the ill, when your creations have lost their flamboyancy in life but not their perseverance.

Throughout the experiences I am taught to feel, Lord; to feel a unity with Thee and with these products of your hand. Thus, in solitude we converse about them—You, as Creator, reminding me of them at the slightest gesture of nature, and I, responding to them with the total response of the created. So thank you for them, Lord, in springtime.

Like the unfolding of spring itself, I am amazed at the unfolding of the lives of my young. The time for walks together now passed, the threshold of shared confidences closing in, I hear less and less the words, "Come on, Mom, let's sit down and talk." I almost wish that I could write again of their early childhood, and that the writing would be current. That, of course, is an understatement, as any parent will agree—or most any parent. I know a few who would rush their children's childhood away, but the majority of us treasure the golden years of our children's youth, when hands were tiny and warm within our own, when sleepy heads rested heavily against the feminine bosom or hung limberly over a strong masculine shoulder. They are indeed golden years in the lives of young families, and I know many such young couples who have treasures in their hands and are so nonchalantly unaware of their richness. Surely theirs are the days of springtime, so impatient in their season.

I find myself wanting to whisper out to those young families to grasp their days of sunshine, to drink fully of their young love, their children, their shiny new homes, because summer comes all too soon after their springtime, and hardly without their awareness follows their winter close behind.

They probably wouldn't hear me; they would continue on in their pursuit of materialistic possessions upon which their culture has placed such value—impatient with jelly smears and wheel marks on floors. Still, those of us in the ancient middle-aged world of our own are not unaware of their world, for we, too, have tasted of their springtime. Now, remembering, we term it "that other spring. . . ."

With the ascent of each new year, we of that older generation are conscious of time's swift flight, and with the passing of each year most of us have accepted the fact that we are never going to be able to accomplish all that we have desired, either in the dimension of the new year ahead or, more probably, in the entirety of our days. At best, we have settled for an incomplete, but in so doing we have not given up our dreams. We bow to the conviction: if not this year, then perhaps next.

How fine a thing to have the desire and the challenge for the incomplete, for the term itself connotes the will to keep our dreams aflame. If we have no motivation, no desire to accomplish, or greater yet, no desire to serve, then we have not taken on an incomplete: we have taken on the rank of failure. But with the incomplete, we exemplify our lives with Robert Frost's woods that are "lovely, dark, and deep"; and with him we too have "miles to go before we sleep."

If we absorbed the lessons from our great teacher, Nature, we would see that she does not curtsey to failure, only to the incomplete. She experiences her dormant season, her time of growth, and then the culmination of her harvest—how wonderful, if youth could ingest her marvelous instruction; how futile, when they have started on a structured course and refuse to accept the detours in the form of difficulties that creep up between the attempt and the achievement of their desired goals; how gratifying, if they could learn that detours designate another direction for clearing a hurdle—not a turning back.

Thoreau had his Walden and I have my tiny back yard pasture. Walking there, I see the tree, how it has grown and shed its shade across the little patch of earth encircled in net wire that has been servant of so many years of use.

First, the plot belonged to Princess the pony when she was young and frisky and required close quarters for bridling. A small shed was built for her there, and the little pasture became her home for a number of years. She was near at hand for a six-year-old and nine-year-old whenever the mood to catch her came upon them, and our front lawn became the center of attraction for the neighborhood youngsters as Princess was taught barrel-racing—using two worn out wash tubs with up-turned rusty bottoms as barrels—and whatever other tricks the illusive world of television rodeo offered for the season.

Through the years the children grew, and Princess was cast aside for wheels and motors, but not quite forgotten, merely turned out into a larger pasture where she has grown old.

"We'll just keep her, Mom," her young owners insisted.

Then the back pasture was empty again, and who can tolerate an empty lot on farm soil? "We'll just move some of the baby calves down there," the children's dad decided.

This spring, there was the little lot—vacant again. Shady on one side now from the huge tree that I planted there years ago, and sunny on the other side from the evening sun, it offered other potentials.

"Let's just make it a garden for Mom. A smaller garden is what she needs now."

Now, as I stir the loose and loamy soil, I agree with that smart fellow who said that "nothing is ever lost, merely changed in some degree," for Princess and the calves have left me a rich residue where I dig and plant whenever the urge to do so strikes me.

Our mockingbird knows I'm there and flits about from the earth to the treetops and back to earth again, eager for the insects that the rich soil offers to him. The catbird darts about as well, ready to start a stir with its peers. The tree beside me offers shade and contentment, growing taller and wider each year, sinking its roots more firmly into the soil: and like me, acquiring a greater cleavage to this place on the land that is home.

Someone said, "Let's have an Earth Day," and so we did. We paused on that day, if only briefly, to pay homage to the land's significance, and then the earth settled down once more to its growing season, its turbulent season passed, its rolling, lashing waters subsided, and spring began. The city-dweller rushes through his work-week to bustle out of the metropolis in search of a quiet spot to pitch his tent, if only for the weekend. The earth reaches out her aqueous arms to his puttering boat, and spreads her grassy regions to his indolent young who come alive with the thought of freedom to roam the earth's wooded areas or to camp by her languid streams.

Then, with his fishing tackle in his hand, man seeks a place of solitude and nestles close to the Mother Earth who bore him without his consent, and finds communion with the seeping message from beneath her crust. Now he knows that he is real—he is no longer just a part of the hub of an office, nor the pusher of buttons in his technical world, but he is a unique part of creation—he has soul and breath and tangible existence. He has dreams that are nearer fulfillment and anxieties that are suddenly lessened.

There, in that quiet spot, he is glad that the earth has had its day. Glad that someone pointed out to him that it was real. He picks up his cluttered cans and deposits them in his garbage bag. Last year he might have tossed them into the clear blue stream at his feet, but not this year: This year, the earth has become part his own; maybe he now shares the thought of a layman friend of mine who stood to pray one day and so wonderfully touched my heart:

"Dear Lord," he began, "We are thankful for this world in which we live. We know that it is good, because You created it. And even though we are aware of the fact that it seems filled with evil at times, still it is ours, and we pray that You will guide us and bless us as caretakers of this land. . . ."

I had never thought of myself in that capacity. Hardly any of us have. We leave the caretaking of God's domain to the gardeners—both in the spiritual and the organic realms. We allow the ministers to do the spading in soil tight with prejudice, for roots run deep in the fertile dust of apathy and indifference. We have long since learned to let our neighbor do as he pleases because it is his right to do so, and we do likewise. If trouble arises, we've learned to say we were looking in the other direction at the time, and didn't see a thing—thus avoiding involvement with our fellowmen.

Organically speaking, we would be reminded at this wonderful season as the earth is seemingly resurrected once more, as the streams and rivers flow at their natural pace, free from the icy weight of winter, that the soil is ours to tend, to preserve; that the earth we tend must be protected from the residue of pesticides which destroy both men and beast; that warnings on herbicides must be heeded; and that penicillin in milk is dangerous to the consumer. All of which relates back to being a conscientious caretaker of God's creation, which in turn relates back to *us*, for indeed, we may be "our brother's keeper." Wasn't it Cain who left us that rhetorical question? Man has pondered it since, with an unsatisfactory answer. Perhaps the question was a warning to future generations, an inauspicious inquiry that, if left unheeded, might answer itself. Like Cain, if we have no regard for our brother's welfare, we, too, may destroy him.

The stainless steel pots on my kitchen range have been turned to low. Their constant jingle reminds me that all is well, the food is cooking, and not too fast. The dishwasher is filling up for the last washing cycle, and the sun is streaming through my kitchen windows. Outside, I hear the hum of the tractor, and I know that my son has been successful in getting the motor going again after the machine's long winter lull. He is a farmer at heart, and spring has a special way of announcing its arrival to young farmers.

On our front lawn a football glides high in the air where my daughter and her jean-clad friends are at play.

I stand at the window and watch, amazed that the tall lithesome fellow jumping from the tractor seat is mine; awed that one of the figures on the lawn in boy jeans is as much at ease there as she is in her bedroom with record players, hair dryers, and giggles past midnight. I am astounded, but pleased; it is another spring, and this one, like all the others, will bring change.

The football slides into the paved road with my daughter right behind it. Not into a highway, nor a street, just a plain asphalt country road, and again I am glad. Thankful for this place that is home, with its fresh air, its solitude, its space for youth to grow and to mature, and answer to the knock of spring. This peaceful home offers a place to listen for spring's beckoning with hearts that are gay and exultant; to bow to its passing with the awareness that another season follows—a fruitful season—when the fruition of a blessed childhood will be harvested; and to anticipate, though not with longing, that last season—the time when spring and summer will have yielded to a hoary eventide.

And may this land, with its lessons in frugality, have taught them to conserve memories as well, memories from that other spring, the spring that is today.